BILLY JOEL®
GREATEST HITS
VOLUME I & VOLUME II

MW01030451

EMI MUSIC PUBLISHING

© EMI Music Publishing, a THORN EMI Company

DISTRIBUTED BY

HAL•LEONARD®
CORPORATION

7777 W. BLUEMOUND RD. P.O. BOX 13819 MILWAUKEE, WI 53213

PIANO MAN

Words and Music by
Billy Joel

SAY GOODBYE TO HOLLYWOOD

Words and Music by
BILLY JOEL

NEW YORK STATE OF MIND

Words and Music by
BILLY JOEL

But I'm tak-in' a Grey-hound on the Hud-son Riv-er line____
But I know what I'm need- in' and I don't want to waste__ more
I don't have an - y rea-sons I've left them all__ be-

time } hind

I'm in a New York____ state of

mind.

D. S. S. al Coda after verse 5

It was so

THE STRANGER

Words and Music by
BILLY JOEL

17

THE STRANGER

Words and Music by
BILLY JOEL

20

THE STRANGER

Words and Music by
BILLY JOEL

25

JUST THE WAY YOU ARE

Words and Music by
BILLY JOEL

32

34

MOVIN' OUT
(ANTHONY'S SONG)

Words and Music by
BILLY JOEL

Moderate 4 (not too slow)

37

39

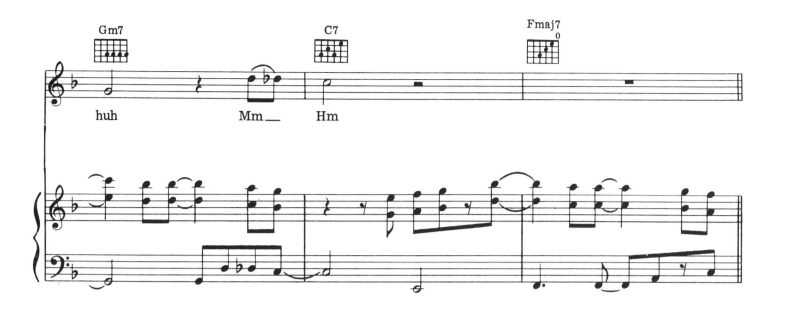

huh Mm — Hm

*Repeat 'til fade
3rd time*

out

2nd time

I'm mov - in'

ONLY THE GOOD DIE YOUNG

Words and Music by
BILLY JOEL

43

SHE'S ALWAYS A WOMAN

Words and Music by
BILLY JOEL

MY LIFE

Words and Music by
BILLY JOEL

(keep it to your-self, it's my_____ life.)

(keep it to your- self it's my_____ life.)

Repeat and fade

YOU MAY BE RIGHT

Words and Music by
BILLY JOEL

BIG SHOT

Words and Music by
BILLY JOEL

70

73

IT'S STILL ROCK AND ROLL TO ME

Words and Music by
BILLY JOEL

Moderately Fast

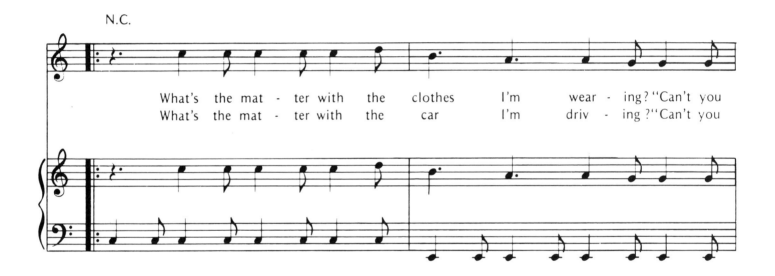

Whats the mat - ter with the clothes I'm wear - ing? "Can't you
What's the mat - ter with the car I'm driv - ing? "Can't you

tell that your tie's too wide?"_____
tell that it's out of style?"_____

78

DON'T ASK ME WHY

Words and Music by
BILLY JOEL

Moderately, in 2

All the ___ wait - ers in your grand ca - fé ___
All your ___ life ___ you had to stand in ___ line. ___

87

ALLENTOWN

Words and Music by
BILLY JOEL

PRESSURE

Words and Music by
BILLY JOEL

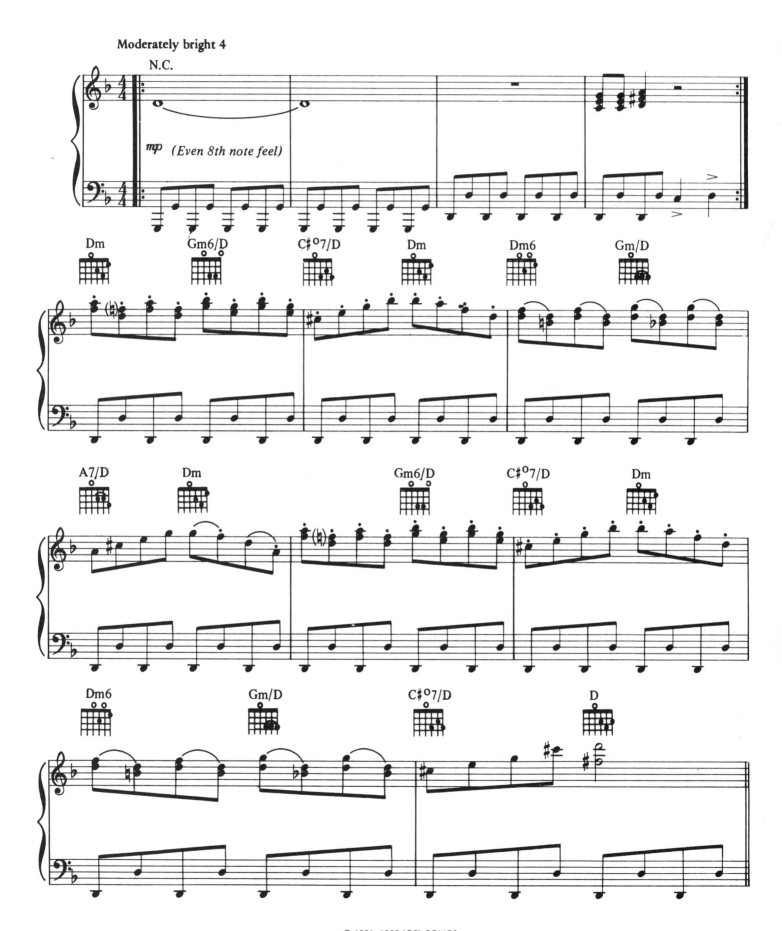

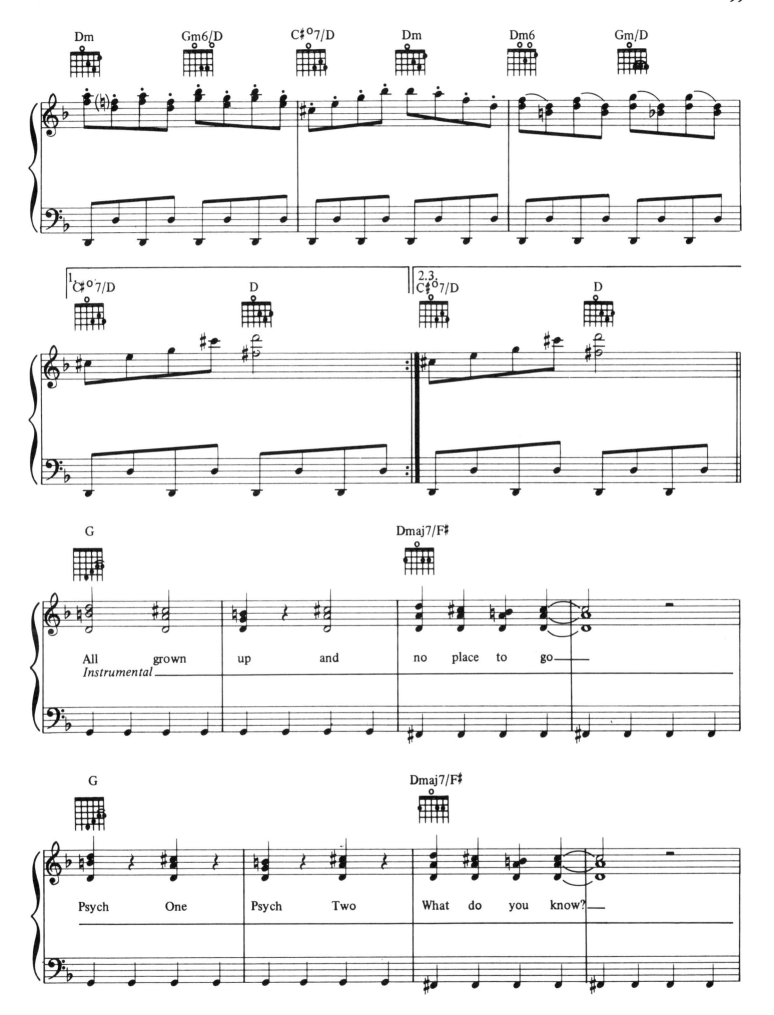

All grown up and no place to go

Instrumental

Psych One Psych Two What do you know?

102

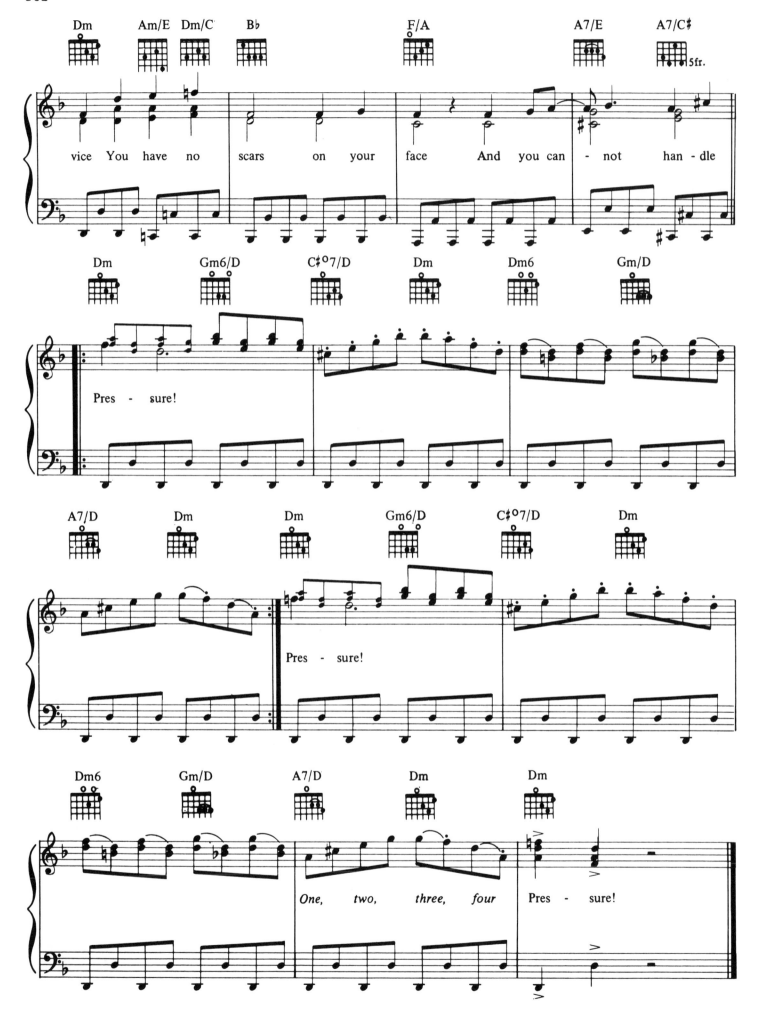

GOODNIGHT SAIGON

Words and Music by
BILLY JOEL

TELL HER ABOUT IT

Words and Music by
BILLY JOEL

Chorus

UPTOWN GIRL

Words and Music by
BILLY JOEL

118

THE LONGEST TIME

Words and Music by
BILLY JOEL

124

YOU'RE ONLY HUMAN
(SECOND WIND)

Words and Music by
BILLY JOEL

Verse 2:
It's not always easy to be living in this
World of pain.
You're gonna be crashing into stone walls
Again and again.
It's alright, it's alright,
Though you feel your heart break.
You're only human, you're gonna have to
Deal with heartache.
Just like a boxer in a title fight;
You got to walk in that ring all alone
You're not the only one who's made
Mistakes.
But they're the only things that you can
Truly call your own. *(To Chorus:)*

Chorus 2:
Don't forget your second wind.
Wait in your corner until that breeze blows in.

Verse 3:
You probably don't want to hear advice
From someone else.
But I wouldn't be telling you if I hadn't
Been there myself.
It's alright it's alright;
Sometimes that's all it takes.
We're only human,
We're supposed to make mistakes.
But I survived all those long lonely days
When it seemed I did not have a friend.
'Cause all I needed was a little faith
So I could catch my breath and face the
World again.

Chorus 3 & 4:
Don't forget your second wind.
Sooner or later you'll feel that momentum kick in.

THE NIGHT IS STILL YOUNG

Words and Music by
BILLY JOEL

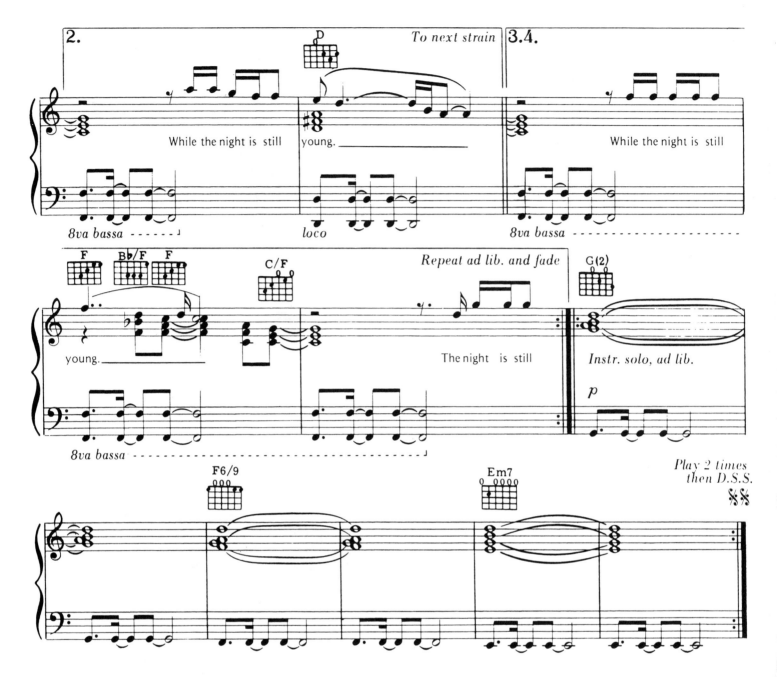

Verse 3:
Rock and Roll music was the only thing I
Ever gave a damn about.
There was something that was missing,
But I never used to wonder why.
Now I know you're the one I need
To make things right again;
And I may lose the battle,
But you're giving me the will to try.

Bridge 2:
Oh . . .
While the night is still young.

Chorus 3:
Because the night is still young,
I've got a lot of catching up I've got to do,
While the night is still young.